GRACE

DAN WINKLER

GRACE

SIMPLY INCREDIBLE
INCREDIBLY SIMPLE

© 2018 by Dan Winkler

All rights reserved. No part of this publication may be reproduced, stored in a retrieval system, or transmitted in any form or by any means without the prior written permission of the author. The only exception is brief quotations in printed reviews.

ISBN-10: 0692151273
ISBN-13: 978-0692151273

Published by d&d publishing
Huntingdon, Tennessee 38344

Printed in the United States of America

Unless otherwise noted, all Scripture quotations are from The Holy Bible, English Standard Version®, copyright © 2001 by Crossway Bibles, a publishing ministry of Good News Publishers. Used by permission. All rights reserved. Scripture quotations marked NKJV are from the *New King James Version*. Copyright © 1979, 1980, 1982 by Thomas Nelson, Inc. Used by permission. All rights reserved.

Cover Design: Josh Feit, Evangela.com

CONTENTS

	Preface	9
1.	The Face of Grace *What Does Grace Really Look Like?*	11
2.	The Showcase of Grace *Can Grace Make That Much Difference?*	31
3.	The Taste of Grace *Why Is Grace So Special?*	57
4.	The Disgrace of Grace *Will Grace Overlook My Behavior?*	73
	Acknowledgment	87
	About the Author	89

DEDICATION

To Diane—the most *gracious* person I know—my high school sweetheart, my precious wife, and the mother of our wonderful sons. Thank you, honey, for being who you chose to be. Every day we are blessed to be together, you inspire me to be a better person. Thank you for giving me your heart. You are amazing, and I love you with all my heart.

PREFACE

Dan Winkler's faith is a pillar of strength. The gracious interaction he has shown throughout his life causes all who know him to pause in admiration as well as self-reflection. If you know Dan well, you have asked yourself if you would be able to be so faithful and gracious. He would be the first to tell you the graciousness he has extended was first given to him by the Gracious Redeemer.

I'm thankful Dan continues to write. This book is short, powerful, and to the point. You will not have to read several slow-moving pages to grasp the context. The first sentence of the first chapter gently, yet immediately, pulls you into a presentation of this beautiful virtue of our loving God—grace.

Every soul desperately needs God's grace. As John Newton said years ago, "Amazing Grace how sweet the sound." But let's face it. As sweet as it is, it is also highly misunderstood. Dan navigates the journey well. In the finale, he addresses two extremes of mishandling God's grace under the chapter entitled "The Disgrace of Grace." He explains that some view God's grace as "No Rules," while others see "Nothing but Rules." Dan's response will challenge us to consider God's feelings. The chapters leading up to this crescendo walk the reader, no matter how little or how exhaustive their understanding of grace, into a thought-provoking and heartwarming journey of this powerful topic. You will better understand grace!

Dan's style of writing is like visiting with him in his living room. When he speaks, you recognize his scholarship which naturally brings interesting insight to any discussion; at the same time, his love for people brings humorous stories and clever expressions that cause the house to be filled with laughter. He and his sweet wife Diane are delightfully hospitable. I know you would enjoy, just as I have, the engaging conversations after dessert.

Because of this, I invite you into a warm and interesting reading about one of the most beautiful gifts ever offered to man. Dan will lead the discussion; be ready to learn and laugh. Be ready to close a chapter feeling like a child who has been offered a special gift. Be ready to feel the need to pray in thanksgiving for God's love. Be ready to be challenged to be a responsible recipient of this amazing gift. Go ahead, turn the page, and begin to wade into *Grace: Simply Incredible, Incredibly Simple*.

— David Shannon
President, Freed-Hardeman University

1

THE FACE OF GRACE
What Does Grace Really Look Like?

What does grace look like? I know. That sounds like a funky question, but walk with me for a minute. See what you think.

When someone asks, "What do you look like?", what are they really talking about? Your fingernails? Fingerprints? Shoe size? Usually, they're talking about your face. Your eyes. Your nose. Your smile. We identify each other by the features of our faces.

Here's a little fun trivia about the unique beauty of your face.

- It has fourteen bones, and the only one that moves is your jawbone, the mandible. (Some of the folks I know talk so much, it's a miracle they haven't worn theirs out. Okay, the devil got the best of me, and I had to throw that one in.)

- It has forty muscles, but only twenty-one of them, the mimetic muscles, are attached to your skin.
- The muscle you chew with is the strongest of your body. (And if you're like me, that's the easiest one to exercise).
- Those cute dimples you wear came from someone in your family, and they're the result of shortened muscles.
- It takes eleven muscles for you to frown and twelve to smile, and the "lines" that furrow across your complexion indicate which of these you use the most. (Dare I ask, "What do your wrinkles say about you?" Have you been happy? Miserable?)
- You can shape and contort your face into about ten thousand different expressions (e.g., anger, excitement, fear, joy).
- As you grow older, you lose bone mass and, guess what? Your face begins to shrink. (Sad it doesn't work that way with our waistlines. I'd like to talk to someone about that when we get to heaven!!)

Nothing is more closely attached to our identities than the features of our faces. It's how we recognize one another. So, to help us identify the incredible features of God's grace, let's see what it looks like.

When a new church was planted in Antioch of Syria, Barnabas was sent to pay them a visit, and this is what the Bible says:

> When he came and *saw the grace* of God, he was glad, and he exhorted them all to remain faithful to the Lord with steadfast purpose.
> Acts 11:22-23; emphasis mine

He "saw" something...something called "grace." But, what did he see?

What does *grace* really look like? I think that's a fair question. We use the word grace in so many different ways. A ballerina is *graceful*. A thoughtful hostess is *gracious*. Before eating, a thankful heart says *grace*. A member of the royal family is addressed as, "Your Grace." If you're tardy paying an insurance premium, your provider will probably offer you a period of *grace*. In Greek mythology, Zeus and Eurynome had three daughters—Aglaea, Euphrosyne and Thalia—known as the three *Graces*.

We use the word *grace* as a synonym for elegance, charm, favor, and benevolence. It's a name we might give to the little girl of our dreams. It's a virtue we want to extend...and receive. But what does grace really look like?

What did Paul have in mind with the words: "[You] are not under law but under grace" (Romans 6:15)? What did he mean when he said, "But by the grace of God I am what I am" (1 Corinthians 15:10)? What are we talking about when we say, "We are saved by grace through faith" (see Ephesians 2:8)?

There are two words that help me, and I'd like to share them with you. See if you don't agree that *grace* is *Simply Incredible & Incredibly Simple*. The two words are:

Devotion — Grace is God's "Devotion" to man, and
Motion — Grace is Jesus in "Motion" with man.

DEVOTION: GRACE IS GOD'S DEVOTION TO MAN

A study of grace respectfully takes us inside the heart of God. It reveals the wonder of his feelings for us. Take the time to read what Paul wrote about it in his letter to the Ephesians:

> God, being rich in *mercy*, because of the great *love* with which he loved us, even when we were dead in our trespasses, made us alive together with Christ—by *grace* you have been saved...so that in the coming ages he might show the immeasurable riches of his *grace* in *kindness* toward us in Christ Jesus. For by *grace* you have been saved through faith.
> Ephesians 2:4-9; emphasis mine

Did you see the words *grace, mercy, love,* and *kindness*? Our faces have three basic features: (a) our eyes, (b) our noses, and (c) our smiles. They help to describe us. Someone might tell me how tall, how large, or how small you are. But I won't really know how to recognize you apart from the details of your face. The color and shape of your eyes. The size of your nose. The warmth of your smile.

The same is true with God's grace. It has three basic features, and the only way we can really come to appreciate it is for us to spend some time with each. They are "mercy," "love," and "kindness."

Mercy is the first basic feature of God's grace. According to Ephesians 2, we are saved by grace because God is "rich in *mercy*" (vv. 4-5, emphasis mine; cf. Luke 6:36).

First, a definition of God's mercy might be helpful. It's the tremendous idea of God experiencing life from our point of view. His heart fuses with our hearts to feel what we feel. And that reveals the softer, more tender side of our heavenly Father (Luke 1:78).

- When we ache over the death of our spouse or child, God is merciful. He's touched by the hole in our soul.

- When we are deprived of our sight, mobility, or strength, God is merciful. He's aware of our frustration.

- When we weep over the shame of our sin, God is merciful. He's drawn to our godly grief.

- When we have to face our mortality, God is merciful. He senses our disappointment.

When life is cruel, God is the "Father of mercies and God of all comfort" (2 Corinthians 1:3-4). When life is hard, we can "draw near to [his] throne of grace, that we may receive mercy and find grace to help" us (Hebrews 4:16). When life is a mess that makes us confess we are less than we ought to be, God is "ready to forgive" because he is "gracious and merciful" (Nehemiah 9:17). Isn't that great?! It makes you want to shout with the psalmist: "I love the Lord, because he has heard my voice and my pleas for mercy" (Psalm 116:1; cf. 119:156). God has feelings for my feelings.

Second, an illustration of God's mercy might also help us to understand and appreciate it. It's found in what the Old Testament calls God's "ark of the testimony" (Exodus 26:33) or "the ark of the covenant of the LORD" (Numbers 10:33; cf. Joshua 4:5).

Look *on top* of this ark. By God's design, two golden angels were placed there with their wings stretched out over the lid. This was called God's "mercy seat" because it's where he would symbolically come and sit while the Jews atoned for their sins (Exodus 25:16-22; 30:6; Leviticus 16:1-2). The imagery is fascinating. Even though God is over the angels (cf. Psalm 148:1-5), he still cared for those he made lower than the angels (cf. Psalm 8:3-6). He sensed their need for forgiveness and provided them with the pageantry of a ritual that proved he felt with them. He was merciful.

Look *inside* the ark. It contained Aaron's budding rod, a copy of the Ten Commandments and—watch it—a pot of gold full of manna (Hebrews 9:4-5). Why manna? It memorialized God's care for Israel while they were in the wilderness (Exodus 16:33-34). They didn't have to go to the mall to buy clothes for the kids or to make a trip to the grocery store for food. God kept their clothes from wearing out and gave them manna to eat every day but Saturday (Deuteronomy 8:3-4). He felt with them and cared for them. Again, he was merciful.

So in summation, we might say that mercy is like God stepping inside our skin to feel what we feel and, then, feel for us. Amazing, right? Yes, amazing grace!

Love is the second basic feature of God's grace. Ephesians 2 goes on to tell us that we are saved by grace because God has *loved* us with a "great love" (vv. 4-5, emphasis mine; cf. Romans 5:8).

First, a definition of God's love might need to be considered. Paul's Greek-speaking friends used a variety of words for love. There was: (a) *erao*, to make love and gratify the flesh, (b) *storgeo*, to love as a family, and (c) *phileo*, to love as a friend. But the word that Paul used in Ephesians 2 is *agapao*, to love and want what's best for the one loved. (*Agapao* is the verb form of the noun *agape*). That's the kind of love God has for us, and it's nothing shy of remarkable. It has the "breadth and length and height and depth" (Ephesians 3:18-19) needed to bless every single one of us…no matter who we are, where we've been, or what we've done.

- Maybe we've been vile and full of guile. His love has the *breadth* needed to embrace us.
- Maybe we've been gone far too long. His love has the *length* needed to reach us.
- Maybe we've been a failure beyond measure. His love has the *height* needed to exalt us.

- Maybe we've been a misfit in some pit of debauchery. His love has the *depth* needed to rescue us.

God, the Father, loves—*agapao/agape*—us and wants what's best for us (John 3:16; Romans 5:6-8). God, the Son, loves—*agapao/agape*—us and wants what's best for us (Galatians 2:20; Revelation 1:5). God, the Holy Spirit, also loves—*agapao/agape*—us and wants what's best for us (Romans 15:30; cf. Philippians 2:1). Their feelings for us are so strong, the Bible even says, "God is love"—*agape* (1 John 4:8).

Second, an illustration of God's love might help us understand and appreciate it. The New Testament gives us a great one. It's found in what we call the Parable of the Prodigal Son (Luke 15:11-32). In this precious story, a selfish young man mistreated his daddy, but when he was broken by sin, he returned to plead for his daddy's help. Incredibly, the daddy not only welcomed his son back, he treated him with the love and respect of royalty. The father of this story represents God. The son represents those of us that have been broken by sin, and, look closer, it's a story about our Father's love.

According to this great story, God loves us when no one else will. The prodigal son was ultimately alone. His "family" wasn't around. He had left them (vv. 11-13). His "friends" weren't around. He was homeless and hungry (vv. 14-16). Even his "firstborn" older brother wasn't there for him. He thought of him as a wasteful whoremonger (vv. 25-30). No one wanted him. No one was there for him…no one but his father (v. 20). That's right! God loves us even when we're unlovable and unloved.

According to this great story, God also loves us even when we don't love ourselves. Listen to the speech the prodigal son prepared for his daddy: "Father, I have sinned against heaven and before you. I am no longer worthy to be called your son. Treat me as one of your hired servants" (vv. 17-19, 21). His self-esteem was shot. His dignity, trashed. His future, ruined. That's not what his father thought. To his daddy, the boy was family and was to be treated with respect (v. 22). To his daddy, the boy was no longer lost. He even replaced his son's humiliation with a happy celebration (vv. 23-24). That's what God's love does for us. He rescues us from our past and loves us even when we don't love or like ourselves.

So in summation, you and I are dear to God. We might be flawed, broken sinners, but God still has deep feelings for us. He's still willing to embrace us with his heart. Okay, say it. "That's amazing!" You're right. It's God's amazing grace!

Kindness is the third basic feature of God's grace. Ephesians 2 also tells us that we are saved by grace because of God's *kindness* or goodness (v. 7, emphasis mine; cf. Romans 11:22).

First, a definition of God's kindness might, once again, be helpful. Kindness is a gentle spirit that does what's right and helps others. It's what Joseph asked of Pharaoh's butler when he predicted the man's release from prison (Genesis 40:9-14). It's what Rahab wanted from the spies when Israel returned to destroy her hometown (Joshua 2:12). It's what Jonathan requested of David after he was given Saul's throne (1 Samuel 20:14-15). It's what David gave to the folks of Jabesh-gilead in return for the care they had given to Saul's decapitated body (2 Samuel

2:4-6). And, thankfully, it's what God offers us. Look at the only other New Testament verses that use the word *kindness* to describe how God treats us:

- His kindness keeps him from losing his temper with us (Romans 2:4).
- His kindness buffers his severity and offers "second chances" (Romans 11:22-23).
- His kindness forgives us and proves he loves us (Ephesians 4:32-5:2).

Feel blessed?! We all should be saying what David said, "Blessed be the LORD, for He has shown me His marvelous kindness" (Psalm 31:21 NKJV). Some of the Old Testament synonyms for this kindness include: "everlasting love" (Isaiah 54:8), "steadfast love" (Isaiah 54:10), "sure love" (Isaiah 55:3), and "faithfulness" (Jeremiah 31:3). The whole idea is that of our being blessed with the attentive feelings of God.

Second, an illustration of God's kindness might also help us to understand and appreciate it. Remember Psalm 23? Can you quote it? Go over it in your mind and see if you can answer these questions.

1. *Who is God called?*—"The LORD" (v. 1). That's spelled with capital letters because it translates God's special name, YHWH, "I am that I am," and it reminds us that we can always rely on his being there for us (Exodus 3:13-14; cf. 6:2-3).

2. *How is God described?*—"My shepherd" (v. 1). Shepherds were those who gave special attention to the needs of others (Ezekiel 34:11-16).
3. *What does God do?* You ready for this? It's remarkable.

With God "looking after us" as our shepherd, we don't have to worry about anything in the future. We can say with David, "I shall not want" (v. 1). Why? (a) God makes us lie down in green pastures and leads us beside still waters. In other words, he offers us the peace of knowing all is well (v. 2). (b) God restores our souls. He puts the pieces of our brokenness back together (v. 3). (c) God also leads us down paths of righteousness for his name's sake. He gives us a sense of direction and purpose (v. 3).

With God "looking over us" as our shepherd, we don't have to be afraid of anyone right now. Like David, we can think about "the deep, dark, shadowy places where death abides" and courageously say, "I will fear no evil" (v. 4). Why? (a) God will be with us. He is there with us (v. 4). (b) God will comfort us. He cares about us (v. 4). (c) God will also prepare a table before us in the presence of our enemies, anoint our heads with oil, and see that our cups overflow. He takes care of us (v. 5).

Now, think about the last verse of this psalm, and see if you can fill in the blanks: "Surely _____ and _____ shall follow me all the days of my life." Here's another way to translate this glorious thought: "Only pleasantry and *kindness* will pursue me all the days of my life" (Psalm 23:6). How many days? Every single one of them. He is always ready to dry the tears from our eyes, carry the burden of our hearts, and lighten the steps of our way.

So in summation, God is our God. God is our shepherd. And God will overshadow us with the kindness of his care. That's right. He's amazing!

Mercy + Love + Kindness = Grace! Amazing grace. God's grace. He feels with us—mercy. He wants what's best for us—love. He gently cares for us—kindness. Grace is God's "Devotion" to man.

MOTION: GRACE IS JESUS IN MOTION WITH MAN

Compassion for others was Jesus' *passion*. With his life, we see the heart of God in motion.

I like to think of the apostle John as Jesus' best friend. You know, "the disciple whom Jesus loved" (John 13:23; 19:26; 20:2; 21:7, 20). Few knew our Lord better, and he went everywhere saying something like this: "We were with Jesus. We knew what he looked like. We were close enough to touch him. We heard what he said, and his words still ring in our ears. We saw what he did, and his miracles still fill our minds with wonder" (read 1 John 1:1-3).

Jesus and John shared something special. That's what makes John's description of Jesus so insightful: He "dwelt among us, and we have seen his glory, glory as of the only Son from the Father, *full of grace and truth*" (John 1:14; emphasis mine). How did Jesus live? He was "full of grace." That means we should be able to study his awesome life and see the mercy, the love, and the kindness of God in motion. And we do. It's breathtaking!

First, Jesus was full of grace, and that means he was full

THE FACE OF GRACE 23

of *mercy*. How many times did he hear someone cry, "Lord, have mercy"? And every single time, he showed them mercy.

Study our Lord's ministry. Remember when his own heart was broken over the murder and mutilation of his cousin, John the Baptizer? He wanted some alone time to talk with God about his feelings. Instead, multitudes found him, and being moved by their needs, he put his own needs on hold. He had compassion for them—felt with them—and helped them (Matthew 14:13-21, esp. v. 14). He was merciful.

When thousands followed Jesus for days and went without anything to eat, he wouldn't send them away hungry. The reason? He didn't want them to faint on their journey home. That's when he fed more than four thousand. He had compassion for them—felt with them—and helped them (Matthew 15:32-39, esp. v. 32). He was merciful.

When our Lord came down from the Mount of Transfiguration, a daddy begged him to help his demon-possessed, tormented son. Jesus didn't disappoint. He cast the demon out of the boy and gave this daddy what he requested. He had compassion for them—felt with them—and helped them (Mark. 9:14-29, esp. v. 22). Again, he was merciful.

Listen to our Lord's message. He encouraged others to feel for people and show compassion. In fact, three of his most-loved parables called for this virtue. For example, there is the Parable of the Unforgiving Servant, in which Jesus taught his disciples to have the "patience," "compassion," and "mercy" needed to forgive (Matthew 18:21-35, esp. v. 27). Then, there is the Parable of the Good Samaritan, in which Jesus taught his followers to have the "compassion" needed to help those who are hurting (Luke 10:25-37, esp. vv. 33, 37). And again, there is the Parable of the Prodigal Son, in which Jesus taught his antagonists—the scribes and Pharisees—to have the "compassion" needed to help those burdened with guilt (Luke 15:1-2, 11-32, esp. v. 20). Jesus constantly felt the pain of others and frequently taught others to do the same. "Be merciful," he would say (Luke 6:36).

Mercy for you and mercy for me too? Think about the compassion Jesus shows us! He is our "merciful and faithful high priest" (Hebrews 2:17). With his help, we get to "draw near the throne of grace [and]…receive mercy" (Hebrews 4:14-16; cf. 7:25). It's hard for me to wrap my mind around all of this. Jesus Christ is sitting right next to Jehovah God (Hebrews 1:3; 10:12; 12:2) and—pause, breathe, wait for it—he's there to serve as our "minister" (Hebrews 8:1-2). He is talking to God face to face "on our behalf" (Hebrews 9:24). Mercy sakes! That's mercy and that's amazing. You're right, it's God's amazing grace!

Second, Jesus was full of grace, and that means he was full of *love*. I just looked through the gospels for the word *love*. Remember, these are the four New Testament books that introduce us to Jesus and the way he lived. Know what I found? The words *love, loved, loves,* or *lovers* at least sixty-six times! And almost two-thirds of those came straight from the lips of Jesus. He believed in love, talked about love, and constantly proved how much he loved.

Stand in the shadows of our Lord's cross. With your mind's eye, reach down and take a handful of the moist, bloodstained sand of Golgotha. Now, let it flow through your fingers and off your hand as if it were sand running through an hour glass. Gently brush away what remains, and look at the crevices of your palm. Can you see them? Red lines drawn by the blood of his love. Listen to the faint echo of his cry, "My God, My God, why…"

Why? Why did Jesus endure the shame and pain of Calvary (Hebrews 12:2-3)? He tells us. "Greater love has no one than this, that someone lay down his life for his friends" (John 15:13). That's why. He "loves us and has freed us from our sins by his blood" (Revelation 1:5). Maybe that's why someone came up with this clever way to spell grace.

G — God's
R — riches
A — at
C — Christ's
E — expense

Sit with those that heard our Lord teach. He practiced what he preached, and he preached what he practiced: love. He taught others: (a) to love their enemies and be nice to them (Matthew 5:44-46); (b) to love God with all their hearts, souls, and minds (Matthew 22:37); (c) to love their neighbors as themselves (Matthew 22:39); (d) to love each other (John 13:34-35; 15:12); and (e) to love him with a love that moved them to do what he said (John 14:15; 21-24).

Love for you and love for me too? Does Jesus love us as much as he loved his own family, friends, and peers? Absolutely. He gave himself to the "suffering of death, so that by the grace of God he might taste death for everyone" (Hebrews 2:9). Everyone. That's you. That's me. Both of us can say what Paul said of Jesus: He "loved me and gave himself for me" (Galatians 2:20). Am I lovable? Sometimes. (Well, that depends on who asks). Am I worthy of his love? Never. But Jesus loves me anyway, and that's incredible. Incredibly amazing. Amazing grace!

Third, Jesus was full of grace, and that means he was also full of *kindness*. It's astounding to see how often Jesus paused to share his life with someone that others might have ignored or deplored.

Watch our Lord take pause and bless someone with a simple touch. On one occasion, two blind men followed Jesus and continually cried out for help (Matthew 9:27-31, esp. v. 29). Picture the scene. They were blind, but they followed. No white canes. (Those weren't introduced until World War I.) No seeing eye dogs. Imagine them stumbling toward walls, running into people, or tripping over uneven places along their path. Sense the desperation of their cry? The verb Matthew used to describe it tells us they sounded like the loud caw of a crow. And, they wouldn't stop. So what did Jesus do? His kindness moved him to touch them and open their eyes to the splendor of God's creation.

When Jesus was on the Mount of Transfiguration, his apostles "fell on their faces…terrified" when they heard the voice of God: "This is my beloved Son, with whom I am well pleased; listen to him" (Matthew 17:1-7, esp. v. 7; cf. Luke 9:28-35). That had to have been frightening. For starters, they were on top of a high mountain. (I hate heights!) Then, they saw the face and clothes of their teacher altered to shine like the sun. And if that wasn't enough to get the juices flowing, they saw two dead men talking to Jesus. About death! Then, all of a sudden, they were overtaken by a bright cloud that must have made them feel like they were inside a smoke-filled house on fire. That's when they heard the voice of God Almighty echo through the cloud and force them to the ground. What did Jesus do? He went over to them and "touched them saying, 'Rise, and have no fear.'" With a heart full of kindness, he reached out to hearts that were full of fear.

To me, one of our Lord's most gracious gestures was outside an obscure village called Nain (Luke 7:11-17, esp. v. 14). There, he met the large funeral procession of a widow's only son. That poor lady had already buried a husband, and she was being forced to walk down that same path of grief behind the casket of her boy. (If you've ever buried one of your children—I have—you know the pain that fills the void of their absence. It never goes away.) That's when Jesus touched the boy's casket, raised him from the dead, and presented him to his mother as a gift of kindness.

We might also turn our attention to the garden of Gethsemane (Luke 22:47-53, esp. v. 51; cf. John 18:10). Remember? Peter drew his sword and severed an ear of Malchus, servant of the high priest. Instead of causing a riot or inciting more violence, Jesus touched the man's ear and completely healed the wound. He showed kindness to one of the many that was being so unkind to him. Now that's amazing.

We might also want to listen to Jesus' call for kindness. Before his familiar words, "Be *merciful*, even as your Father is merciful," he extended this mind-boggling challenge: "*Love* your enemies...and you will be sons of the Most High, for he is *kind* to the ungrateful and the evil" (Luke 6:35-36, emphasis mine). Do what? To whom? Wait a minute. Maybe you saw it, but I missed it at first. All three features of grace are referenced in this one text. It tells us to be "merciful," to "love," and to be "kind" like our heavenly Father. Jesus taught others to be kind and, yes, full of grace.

Kindness for you and kindness for me too? The "Lord is good" [*chrestos*, "kind"] to us and makes it possible for us to be "a chosen race, a royal priesthood, a holy nation, a people for [God's] own possession" (1 Peter 2:3, 9). Red, yellow, black, or white, we can all be precious members of his "chosen race." Rich or poor, common or colossal, we can all be "royal." No clergy. No laity. No hierarchy. We can all be part of his special "priesthood." Whether we live in America, Africa, or Antartica, if we're cleansed by his blood, we can belong to a "holy nation" with our citizenship in heaven. We belong to God. We're his people because his Son has been so good, so kind, so amazingly full of grace.

What does grace look like? Mercy. Love. Kindness. That's it, and it's wonderful!

I'd like to ask you to do something for me before

we close. It might not seem relevant, but try it anyway. Okay?

Would you take a moment and go look at yourself in a mirror? It doesn't have to be one of those make-up mirrors that magnifies your bloodshot eyes. Just a regular mirror will do. Go ahead, I'll wait right here. I know it sounds silly, but take just a minute to briefly look at yourself. Not one of those casual—"Is all of my hair in place?"—glances. Stare at yourself with your mind's eye. Take the whole minute.

If you're looking for grace, you'll find it in those of us that have been blessed by the *mercy* of God's forgiveness, the *love* of God's acceptance, and the *kindness* of God's care. I hope it's what you see in the face of the one that was smiling back at you in the mirror. Was it the face of someone that has been touched by the heart of God and changed by the redemptive work of his Son?

That's right. "The Face of Grace" is—or it can be—your face.

2

THE SHOWCASE OF GRACE
Can Grace Make That Much Difference?

My youngest brother lives in Tuscaloosa, Alabama. He's a graduate of the university, a retired faculty member, and as you would expect, a huge University of Alabama football fan. During one of our visits, I asked if we might be able to see the NCAA National Championship trophies the school has on display.

WOW! I've never seen anything like that. We were given a guided tour of a multi-storied building. What we saw made me feel like a little boy with his pockets full of quarters in a candy store.

- There were SEC championship trophies and rings on display behind glass and, with them, a large picture of an athlete that made contributions to a championship season.

- There were Heisman trophies (you know, the one

awarded to the most outstanding football player in the nation) perched on pedestals to remind you of the special talent that has come through the university.

- There were plaques of former players that have been inducted into the College Football Hall of Fame and shadow-boxes packed with the pictures of those that have been named to All-American teams through the years.

- There were replicas of other trophies awarded each year and, behind each, a list of the Alabama athletes that have won that award…along with a picture of the most recent recipient from the university. They include: (a) the Walter Camp Player of the Year Award, given to the best player of the year; (b) the Butkus Award, given to the best linebacker of the year; (c) the Doak Walker Award, given to the best running back of the year; (d) the Johnny Unitas Golden Arm Award, given to the best fourth-year quarterback of the year; and (e) the Vince Lombardi Rotary Trophy, awarded to the year's most outstanding offensive or defensive lineman. (That one is my favorite. It's a solid piece of granite, and the symbolism is hard to miss. The line of scrimmage is where the game is won or lost.)

- Then, there was the grand prize: the National Championship trophies. I've seen them on TV, but this time, I got to see one up close and personal. It sets on a two-tiered pedestal inside a protective tube of thick glass. On either side, there's a tower of crimson "Bama" football helmets, one for each championship they've won. On each helmet, there's a white number indicating the specific year they were national champs. Impressive!

When we read through the Bible, we are blessed to look inside another trophy case. We might call it "The Showcase of God's Grace." It displays something more amazing than anything you will ever see in this world. One literary portrait after another. Hearts that were moved. Lives that were changed. Destinies that were altered. They are the "trophies" of God's heart.

Remember what Paul had to say about himself when he reflected back to his own conversion? His picture is on display inside God's "Showcase of Grace."

> [T]hough formerly I was a blasphemer, persecutor, and insolent opponent. But…*the grace of our Lord overflowed for me* with the faith and love that are in Christ Jesus. The saying is trustworthy and deserving of full acceptance, that Christ Jesus came into the world to save sinners, of whom I am the foremost. But I received mercy for this reason, *that in me*, as the foremost, Jesus Christ *might display* his perfect patience as an example.
> 1 Timothy 1:13-16; emphasis mine

To prove that the grace of God really can make a difference, let's look at four other "trophies" that were touched and blessed by the amazing grace of God. Two will come from the Old Testament and two from the New Testament:

1. Rahab—from the "madam of Jericho" to the "manger of Jesus,"
2. Samson—from a "narcissistic heel" to a "national hero,"
3. Mary Magdalene—from a "grave plight" to the "grave site" of Jesus, and
4. Simon Peter—from an "impetuous fisherman" to a "precious fisher of men."

RAHAB

At one time, she was somebody's little girl. I wonder if she ever "played house," helped her momma cook, or listened to her daddy tell bedtime stories. Reckon she ever had something like a "hope chest" for her dreams of a wedding, a happy home, and a house full of children?

Well, she got the house, but it probably wasn't the one of her childhood dreams. It was frequented by men. It was a brothel. And that's how we are first introduced to "a prostitute whose name was Rahab" (Joshua 2:12). Thankfully, she didn't stay in that house or in that profession, and that's why we find her picture inside God's "Showcase of Grace." Here's part of her story:

Rahab was a very *worldly* person. I know. Some have tried to make her a legitimate business woman. They tell me she was an "inn keeper," but that just won't pass the integrity test. See

THE SHOWCASE OF GRACE

what you think.

*First, Rahab's **vocation** tells us she was not a very nice person.* When Joshua dispatched two spies to Jericho, they ended up in the house of Rahab and "lodged there" (Joshua 2:1). The Hebrew word used for *lodge* is also translated *lie with*, and it carries the idea of people lying down to have sex (e.g., Leviticus 18:22; 20:3; Deuteronomy 22:22; 2 Samuel 11:11). Where did that happen? In the house of Rahab. She appears to have been a "madam" for one of the city's houses of ill repute.

*Second, Rahab's **identification** tells us she was not a very nice person.* The Holy Spirit frequently identified folks by their occupations. Amos was "a herdsman and a dresser of sycamore figs" (Amos 7:14). Peter and Andrew were "the fishermen" (Mark 1:16; Luke 5:2). Lydia was "a seller of purple goods" (Acts 16:14). Rahab…well, Rahab was "the prostitute" (Hebrew *zonah*, "one who engaged in illicit sexual intercourse"). And she was repeatedly identified this way (Joshua 6:17, 22, 25). Of interest, the verb form of this Hebrew word *zonah* is translated, "began to whore with" in Numbers 25:1. So, what does that say about Rahab?

*Third, Rahab's **description** tells us she was not a very nice person.* Twice in the New Testament, she is called "Rahab the prostitute" (Greek *porne*; cf. *porn*) or, to be more literal, "Rahab, the harlot for hire" (Hebrews 11:31; James 2:25). In Old Testament times, there were two kinds of prostitutes. (a) There were religious prostitutes who engaged in sex as a professional devotee to some pagan god. One of these women or men was called a *qedeshah*, a "cult prostitute" (Deuteronomy 23:17;

1 Kings 14:24; 15:12; 22:46; Hosea 4:14). (b) There were also licentious prostitutes who sold a use of their body to gratify the sexual urge of another. A woman was called a *zonah*, a "prostitute," and a man known as a *kelev*, a "dog" (Genesis 34:31; Leviticus 19:29; Deuteronomy 23:18). Rahab fit into the latter of these two categories. She made her living serving up sex to men that came to her house. Yes. I agree. That's disgusting! But that's who she was…what she did.

The Old Testament book of Proverbs had a lot to say about someone like Rahab. And it's not all that pretty:

- Harlots are like a sharp sword that will rip you to pieces, destroy your life, and damn your soul (Proverbs 5:3-8).
- Harlots are cheap…but they will cost you a fortune (Proverbs 6:26; 29:3).
- Harlots are shamelessly seductive and painfully destructive (Proverbs 7:10-23).
- Harlots are like a deep hole in that you can't escape from the consequences of their touch (Proverbs 23:27-28).

And look at what the Old Testament says about houses like the house of Rahab: "Her house is the way to hell" (Proverb 7:27 NKJV). Thankfully, that's not where we leave Rahab.

Rahab became a *wonderful* person. The first time she's mentioned in the Bible, she's a harlot. The last time she is mentioned, she is "justified" (James 2:25). The path from one to the other makes for a beautiful study of a journey that involved several steps.

*Step #1: Rahab **protected** the spies of Israel (Joshua 2:2-7).* Walls have ears. It's hard to keep a secret. So when Joshua's two spies came to Jericho, word of their presence and purpose made its way to the city's king. How did the king's officials know they could go to Rahab's house to find the spies? Someone in Rahab's neighborhood or someone in her brothel—another prostitute, a "customer"—had to have been the tattletale. But when the king's embassage came, Rahab hid the spies and lied about their presence. (Okay, she shouldn't have lied, but she did, and we need to be honest about her being dishonest). Then, she sent the king's men on a wild goose chase away from the spies (Joshua 2:2-7). Why did she dare to do that? Keep reading.

*Step #2: Rahab **accepted** the God of Israel (Joshua 2:8-13).* Before she sent the spies away, she made a request that reveals a deep faith in God.

> I know that the LORD has given you the land, and that the fear of you has fallen upon us, and that all the inhabitants of the land melt away before you. For we have heard how the LORD dried up the water of the Red Sea before you when you came out of Egypt, and what you did to the two kings of the Amorites who were beyond the Jordan, to Sihon and Og, whom you devoted to destruction...[T]he LORD your God, he is God in the heavens above and on the earth beneath. Now then, please swear to me by the LORD that, as I have dealt kindly

with you, you also will deal kindly with my father's house, and give me a sure sign that you will save alive my father and mother, my brothers and sisters, and all who belong to them, and deliver our lives from death.

Joshua 2:9-13

Did you see what she called God? "LORD" (Hebrew *YHWH*). That's the covenant name God gave to himself for Moses and Israel to use (Exodus 6:2-7). For Rahab to use this name—and do so four times—is remarkable. She came from a pagan, polytheistic background (cf. Deuteronomy 12:29-31), but, here, she spoke of her faith in the one and only true God of Israel: "[T]he LORD your God, he is God in the heavens above and on the earth beneath." The writer of Hebrews reminds us that she did what she did "[b]y faith" (Hebrews 11:31), and here, we see her faith in the power of God dividing the Red Sea for Israel (Exodus 14-15) and in the care of God fighting the Amorites for Israel (Numbers 21:21-35). It was a faith that compelled her to help the spies and request help from the spies.

*Step #3: Rahab was **protected** by the army of Israel (Joshua 6:1-25a).* Her request was granted. Jericho was taken in dramatic fashion. Israel encircled the city once a day for six days. Then, on the seventh day, they marched around the city seven times, the priests blew trumpets, the people shouted, the wall of the city fell, and everyone living inside was slashed or impaled by the sword. Only Rahab, her possessions, and all that were with her in her house were spared.

*Step #4: Rahab was **accepted** by the people of Israel (Joshua*

6:25b). The divine record offers us a little caveat that we might overlook if we're not really careful. It says, "Rahab the prostitute and her father's household and all who belonged to her, Joshua saved alive. And she has lived in Israel to this day." She lived with Israel and became one of them. Her story gets even better. She married a man of Judah named Salmon, and they had a boy they named Boaz (Matthew 1:2-5). Do you know what that means? Rahab was the great-great-great-grandmother of king David. Even more impressive, she is one of only five women mentioned in the genealogy of Jesus Christ (Matthew 1:1-17). (By the way, she is also one of only two women mentioned in Hebrews 11, "Faith's Hall of Fame.") She went from being a madam in Jericho to the lineage of Jesus, who was born and placed in a manger.

How's that for a changed life?! And it was the result of men swearing by the LORD that a woman would be shown "kindness" (Hebrew *chesed*, one of the key components of grace (Joshua 2:12; 6:22, 25). Grace made a huge difference in Rahab's life.

SAMSON

Some people never grow up. They do what they want to do and say what they want to say, "come what may." They're MYopic. They live like they're on a high from too much vitamin "I." Everything has to be something about them because, after all, they're supposed to be the center of everyone else's universe.

Samson was that kind of guy. He was a Danite by birth (Judges 13:1-3, 24-25) and a Nazirite by divine order (Judges

13:4-5), and he married a Canaanite just because it's what he wanted to do (Judges 14:1-2). After we read of his birth, the Bible takes us straight to his life as an adult…and he was a spoiled brat.

> [He] went down to Timnah, and at Timnah he saw one of the daughters of the Philistines. Then he came up and told his father and mother, "I saw one of the daughters of the Philistines at Timnah. Now get her for me as my wife." But his father and mother said to him, "Is there not a woman among the daughters of your relatives, or among all our people, that you must go to take a wife from the uncircumcised Philistines?" But Samson said to his father, "Get her for me, for she is right in my eyes."
> Judges 14:1-3

He was a narcissistic adult juvenile that had to have his way. Momma and daddy pampered him and facilitated his selfish pettiness. That's the man we meet when we're first introduced to Samson. But the rest of his story is why his picture has been placed inside God's "Showcase of Grace." Here's the bulk of his story:

Samson lived as an extremely *self-serving* jerk. His name means "sunshine" or "sunny," but he didn't live up to it. He was sullen, spiteful, and selfish, and he proved to be his own worst enemy. Here are three words we might use to encapsulate most of his life:

*First, Samson was an **angry** person (Judges 14).* He married his Canaanite beauty, and they gave a party for thirty of her heathen friends. At that party, Samson posed a riddle and a wager, attempting to impress his peers. If his guests answered the riddle within seven days, he would give them thirty linen garments and thirty changes of clothing. If not, they would give him the same. At the end of seven days, the guests were stumped. So they got "Mrs. Samson" to betray her husband and get them the answer. Samson was so outraged, he murdered thirty other Philistines, stripped their corpses, and paid off his wager. When he finished, the Bible says that "in hot anger he went back up to his father's house" (v. 19). Hot is from the Hebrew verb that means "to burn." *Anger* translates the Hebrew noun for *nose*, probably because the nose can dilate when one is full of rage. Now, look at the word picture. Samson's nose flared and his heart was set on fire with such rage he ran home to mommy and daddy...no doubt, to pout.

*Second, Samson was an **avenging** person (Judges 15).* When he finally calmed down, he returned to his father-in-law and claimed the rights of a husband. There, he found that his wife had been given to the best man of their wedding. (Bad move! You don't want to stir the ire of someone that has the body of a man, the strength of a superhero, and the temperament of a toddler.) That's when Samson caught three hundred foxes and tied their tails together with a torch between each pair of tails. He lit the torches, released the foxes, and set the Philistine countryside ablaze. Grain fields. Vineyards. Olive groves. They were all torched. The Philistines responded with a fire of their own. They burned Samson's wife and father-in-law to death, and Samson's reaction is best described in his own words: "If this is what you do, I swear I will be avenged on you, and after that I will quit" (v. 7). He was a man of his word. He slaughtered them all with the fury of a man out to revenge his losses.

*Third, Samson was an **adulterous** person (Judges 16).* Extramarital sex was a way of life to this fellow. No surprise. Being as selfish as he was, he had a hard time controlling his libido. For example, we read of his chance encounter with "a prostitute" on one occasion (vv. 1-3). Then, there was his long-standing, self-destructive affair with Delilah (vv. 4-21). Her name might have meant "dainty one," but she was a force to reckon with. And it cost Samson his hair, his strength, his freedom, his eyes, his self-respect, and…his life.

Not a pretty picture is it? But that's the *old* Samson. Wait till you meet the *new* Samson. We have to wait to the last day and the last moments of his life, but it's worth the wait.

Samson died as an extremely *self-giving* champion. As with Rahab, when we first meet Samson, we're not all that impressed. But the last time he's mentioned in the Bible, he's a hero, like Gideon, David, Samuel, and the prophets (Hebrews 11:32). What made the difference? Listen to his last words. It's a prayer. He was being made sport of by the Philistines in one of their temples when he asked to be led to the pillars supporting the temple. Before he pushed the pillars away—and "brought down the house"—he talked to God.

> O Lord GOD, please remember me and please strengthen me only this once, O God, that I may be

avenged on the Philistines for my two eyes...Let me die with the Philistines.

>   Judges 16:28-30

In his last moments, Samson prayed and was more submissive to God than he had been (v. 28). When hundreds of Philistines gathered to worship Dagon, their god of grain, he turned to his God and prayed: "O Lord GOD, please remember me." Before this moment, we read of Samson praying only one other time. Only once—and in that prayer, he complained because God didn't have something for him to drink after a great battle...as if God owed him something for all he had done (Judges 15:18). But his last words took on a different tone. He didn't complain like someone entitled to God's attention. No, he asked to obtain God's assistance.

In his last moments, Samson prayed and was more aware of God than he had been (vv. 28-29). Three chapters chronicle this man's sad life (Judges 14-16). Read them. He spoke of "God" only once, and even then, he was talking about himself (Judges 16:17). Samson was too busy thinking about himself to have any thoughts of God. His heart was so full of himself, there was no room for God. Even when he prayed that one prayer we mentioned earlier, he didn't call God by name. He just cried out something like an awful, "Hey, you..." (Judges 15:18). But his last words were far more respectful. They employ three different words for God: *Lord* (Hebrew *Adonay*, "Master"), *GOD* (Hebrew *YWHW*, "I am that I am"), and *God* (Hebrew *Elohim*, "Gods," the respectful and majestic plural of *El*).

In his last moments, Samson prayed and was more dependent on God than he had been (v. 30). His prayer continued: "O Lord GOD, please remember me and please strengthen me only this once, O God…Let me die with the Philistines." During his life, hundreds fell victim to his physical strength and emotional weakness. Thirty in Judges 14. Who knows how many in the early verses of Judges 15? Then, a thousand more in the latter part of Judges 15. That's when he bragged:

> With the jawbone of a donkey, heaps upon heaps,
> with the jawbone of a donkey have I struck down a
> thousand men.
>
> Judges 15:16

But in the last moments of his life, Samson was completely dependent on God: "O Lord GOD, please…please…O God." The result? He pushed away pillars supporting the Philistines' temple, and three thousand more enemies of God were killed (Judges 16:26-27, 30a). And because he came to believe in and rely on God, "the dead whom he killed at his death were more than those whom he had killed during his life" (Judges 16:30b).

As we mentioned earlier, the last time we read about Samson, he's listed in Hebrews 11, "Faith's Hall of Fame." This chapter is the one about those who had a faith that saved their souls (Hebrews 10:39). Can you believe it? Samson was saved?! He went from a self-absorbed narcissist to a saved champion because our God is a God of second chances, a God of grace.

MARY

All sorts of crazy stuff has been reported about this good woman. For centuries, some have tried to make her the immoral woman that washed Jesus' feet with her tears (Luke 7:36-50). That may be because we read of that woman just before we are introduced to Mary (Luke 8:1-2). But there's absolutely no evidence that the two were one and the same. More recent imaginations have tried to make her the consort of Jesus. Can you imagine?! She is never referenced as his wife, nor he as her husband. And, since he lived without sin (2 Corinthians 5:21; Hebrews 4:15), their relationship couldn't have been anything but platonic.

Here's what we do know: First, we know that Mary was a woman. That was one strike against her in Jesus' day. Back then, women weren't that important. Rabbis refused to teach them and would pray prayers of gratitude for not being born a woman. They didn't even want to talk to women in public (John 4:27). Second, we know that Mary was with Jesus at the beginning of his Galilean preaching (Luke 8:1-2). That means she was with him for almost his entire ministry. Third, we know that Mary was called "Magdalene" (Luke 8:2), and that's probably because she was from Magdala, a city west of the Sea of Galilee (Luke 8:2; cf. Matthew 15:39). Fourth, we know that she and many other women "provided for" (Greek *diakoneo*, "served tables" for) Jesus and his apostles during their ministry (Luke 8:3). Oh yeah, there's one more thing. We know that Mary had a past. She had a very dark past that helps us see why her picture ended up in God's "Showcase of Grace." Here's where her story begins:

Mary Magdalene was, at one time, *possessed* of demons. She's described as someone "from whom seven demons had gone out" (Luke 8:2). Demons? Elsewhere, they're known as "unclean spirits" (Mark 7:25; cf. Matthew 15:22) that transmigrated into this world and took up residence in people's bodies. Mary's body was home to seven of them. Seven! Seven of Satan's filthy messengers lived inside her body. Think of what that means.

*First, that means Mary was **controlled**.* She was controlled by the devil. He was "ruler of the demons" (Matthew 12:24-27). He's the one that dispatched these wicked minions of darkness (cf. Ephesians 6:12) into this world and into the lives of men (Matthew 9:32), women (Luke 8:2), boys (Matthew 17:14-18), or girls (Mark 7:26). Mary was one of his victims.

*Second, that means that Mary was **consumed**.* She was possessed of seven demons. In Hebrew literature, seven was a symbol of "perfection" or "completion." That, alone, speaks to Mary's plight. She was completely possessed. But symbolism set aside, remember the story Jesus told about a demon that left its host, only to return with seven more. Jesus said "the last state of that person was far worse than the first" (Luke 11:24-26). That's what Mary had to deal with in real life. Seven demons lived inside her body…a fate worse than words can express.

*Third, that means that Mary was **corrupted**.* Demons were savage. The psychosomatic disorders they caused were catastrophic: e.g., violent convulsions (Mark 1:23-26), insanity (Mark 5:1-15), seizures, and the inability to speak or hear

(Mark 9:17-18, 25-26). The only other example of "multiples" possessing a person was that poor fellow of Gadara. He was turned into a fierce, homeless, ultra-strong, naked madman that terrorized his neighbors by screaming and cutting himself when they came around the cemetery he haunted (Mark 5:1-9; cf. Matthew 8:28; Luke 8:26-28). Awful. Right?! We can only imagine what the seven living inside Mary forced her to do. But that was B.C., *Before Christ* came into her life.

Mary Magdalene became one of the *best* of all disciples. Twice, she's described as a demoniac. But Jesus "healed" (Greek *therapeuo*, cf. *therapeutic*) her by forcing all seven demons to leave her body (Luke 8:2; cf. Mark 16:9). Mary owed Jesus her new life. (Don't we all!) And she proved to be one of his most appreciative, committed followers.

Mary was one of the last to leave Jesus' side when he died. She stood "by" (more literally, "near") his cross along with his mother, his aunt, his best friend, and the wife of a man named Clopas (John 19:25-27). Then, when they left, they couldn't leave. They continued to watch (Greek *theoreo*, cf. *theorize*) from a distance (Matthew 27:50-56). They tried to put together all that was happening. They saw him draw his last breath and hang lifeless from the nails in his hands and feet. They felt the earth quake under their feet and saw the rocks split open as if all of nature convulsed over the death of its creator. They were probably too far away to hear the centurion say, "Truly this was the Son of God," but they knew that anyway. Mary was there to witness every bit of that. She was with him toward the beginning of his ministry, and she was with him to the bitter end.

Mary was one of the first and one of the last to be with the body of Jesus when it was buried. She "saw where he was laid," making sure that everything was as it should be (Mark 15:46-47; cf. Luke 23:55). Then, she sat down close to the opening while the men finished up (Matthew 27:59-61). Of interest, she was also one of the first to return to the tomb early Sunday morning (Matthew 28:1; Mark 16:1; John 20:1).

Mary was also one of the very first persons to see Jesus after his resurrection. To me, Mary's encounter with our risen Lord is one of the most tender scenes in scripture. She was sitting outside what she thought was his violated tomb, weeping out loud like a baby. Jesus appeared to her, and at first, she didn't recognize him. (Don't ask me why. Wish I knew.) He asked her two questions: "Why are you crying? Who are you looking for?" Then, he spoke a word that touches my heart every time I read it. He said, "Mary" (John 20:11-16). He called her by name!

Of interest, with only one exception, every time Mary Magdalene is mentioned in a list of people, she's mentioned first. That's a gesture that implies her place of significance in the life of our Lord. Few loved him more. Few were changed more by his kindness, his amazing grace. It really made a difference in her life, didn't it?!

PETER

Some people are easy to love. Others, you have to work hard just to like. To me, Peter fits into the latter. I don't mean to be ugly. He just seems to have one of those strong personalities

THE SHOWCASE OF GRACE

that would have been hard to get along with.

He's one with multiple names: Simon, his Greek name; Cephas, his Aramaic name; Peter ("rock"), his nickname; and Simeon, his Hebrew name (John 1:42; Acts 15:14). You can't help but wonder if he had multiple personalities, one for each name! No, he didn't. I just said that in jest because his life is a study of such contrasts. Before Jesus' resurrection, he looks like a different person almost every time we turn a page of scripture. Hot. Cold. Courageous. Cowardly. Ready to fight. Taking flight. But, what was he like after Jesus' resurrection? Ah, that's why his picture is in God's "Showcase of Grace."

Peter repeatedly *disappointed* Jesus. Remember the gunslinger in those old Hollywood westerns? They were "quick on the draw." Well, Peter was "quick on the flaw." He was constantly messing up for at least three reasons.

*First, Peter was **impulsive**.* Time and again, he'd open his mouth and insert his foot. Or, he would leap before he looked. Remember when the apostles were battling to stay alive at sea? Jesus came walking on the water and identified himself. Peter's the one that said, "Lord, if it is you, command me to come to you on the water." What if it hadn't been Jesus? Ever thought of that? Oh, by the way, to his credit he did step out of the boat, but Jesus ended up having to rescue him and reprimand him for his doubts (Matthew 14:22-31).

On the Mount of Transfiguration, it was Peter that impulsively had to say something about Jesus, Moses, and Elijah being there together. He suggested that tabernacles of respect be made for all three, and he no sooner got that idea out of his mouth than God corrected him, "This is my beloved Son…listen to him." Ouch!

When Jesus was arrested, where was Peter? Remember, he's the one that impulsively promised to die for Jesus (Matthew 26:35). Instead, he followed "at a distance…to see the end" (Matthew 26:35, 58). Where? Why? Really?!

*Second, Peter was **abrasive**.* He was the type that would invade your space and get in your face. For example, on one occasion, Jesus told a parable, and Peter said to him, "Explain the parable to us" (Matthew 15:15). The verb he used for *explain* is an imperative, a command. Peter dared to command an explanation from Jesus. Man, that's brazen!

We see something similar when Jesus encouraged his disciples to resolve conflicts and forgive those that sinned against them. Peter's the one that asked, "How often do I have to do that?" (Matthew 18:15-21).

On another occasion, they were surrounded by "crowds." (Don't miss the plural.) Folks were everywhere when a woman came and touched Jesus, hoping to be healed from a twelve-year blood disorder. Jesus asked, "Who was it that touched me?" Peter's reply went something like this: "Are you kidding me?! Who touched you?! We can barely move with all these people around, and you want to know who touched you?!" (Luke 8:43-45). That's cold.

There's also the time Peter took Jesus apart and commenced to "take him apart." Yes, you read that right. Peter rebuked Jesus (Mark 8:31-32). Can you imagine escorting Jesus into a private corner, only to scold him for teaching what he taught? That was

Peter. By the way, Jesus didn't leave that unaddressed. He counterpunched with a rebuke of his own: "Get behind me, Satan! For you are not setting your mind on the things of God, but on the things of man" (Mark 8:33).

*Third, Peter was **defensive**.* Where I grew up, we'd say, "He could get his hackles up in heartbeat hurry." For example, Jesus predicted that all the apostles would scatter the night of his arrest, and Peter wouldn't have any part of that idea. "Though they all fall away (Greek *scandalizo*, "become a scandal") because of you, I will never fall away," was his response (Matthew 26:31-33). That was the same occasion Peter was told he would deny the Lord. How'd that turn out?

Do you remember his reaction to Jesus washing the apostles's feet? It went something like this: "You're not going to wash my feet." "Peter, if I don't wash yours, you can't be part of me." "Then, Lord, give me a bath" (John 13:1-11). The guy was constantly having to defend some crazy thing he said. Maybe that's why he's thought to be the "foot-in-mouth" disciple.

Here's another: The Lord told the apostles that one of them would betray him. So Peter got John to do his dirty work. He motioned for John and told him to ask Jesus who it was going to be (John 13:21-26). Why did he have to know? Reckon he had doubts about himself? I wonder if he was trying to defend himself to himself. Just saying… You see, that same night, Peter is the one that tried to singlehandedly take on an army with his sword, only to be scared to death by the question of a little girl hours later (John 18:10, 15-17). Still, all of that was before our Lord's resurrection and the change that came over this man. It's only part of his story.

Peter became someone that *pointed* people to Jesus. He turned out to be one of the most influential church leaders of his day. He's the one that took the lead in finding a replacement for Judas Iscariot (Acts 1:15-26). He's the one that defended his brethren on the day of Pentecost and led the charge of preaching Jesus (Acts 2:14-40). He's the one that challenged the deception and greed of Ananias and Sapphira (Acts 5:1-11). And Peter is the one Herod wanted to execute to become more popular among the Jews (Acts 12:1-4). The strong personality Jesus nicknamed "the Rock" became one of the key personalities God used to launch his cause. Look at the difference grace made in his life:

Peter pointed people to Jesus in his preaching. Take the time to read the sermon he preached in Acts 2:22-38. Read it out loud to yourself just for the fun of it. Listen for his references to: (a) the miraculous "confirmation" of Jesus (v. 22), (b) the vicarious "crucifixion" of Jesus (v. 23), (c) the victorious "resurrection" of Jesus (vv. 24-32), (d) the glorious "exaltation" of Jesus (vv. 33-35), and (e) that famous "conclusion" we need to make about Jesus: "God has made him both Lord and Christ" (v. 36). Isn't that something?! Elsewhere in Acts, he went on to preach about Jesus as "Lord" (2:36; 10:36; 11:17), "Christ" (2:36, 38; 3:6, 20; 4:10; 5:42; 10:36, 48; 11:17), the special "servant" of God (3:13; 4:27, 30), the "cornerstone" of God's plan for man (4:11), and the "anointed" of God (10:38). He changed from a man that denied knowing Jesus into a man that wanted everybody to know about Jesus.

THE SHOWCASE OF GRACE 53

Peter pointed people to Jesus in the letter we call 1 Peter. He wrote this letter to brethren that had been forced to leave their homes and start life over in a foreign country we now call Turkey (1 Peter 1:1). He used the word *suffer* seventeen times. (It's found more in this book of the New Testament than any other.) Synonyms like *grieved, trials, harm, troubled, slandered,* and *revile* are also sprinkled throughout the letter. Peter wanted to help these folks, and he did so by encouraging them to think more about Jesus. The Lord's personal name, Jesus, or his title, Christ, is used an average of once every three-and-a-half verses. He wrote about: (a) the "resurrection" of Jesus and made sure everyone knew it's the reason we have the hope of heaven and the assurance of being saved when we're baptized (1 Peter 1:3-4; 3:21), (b) the "revelation" of Jesus and the grace he will bring when he comes again (1 Peter 1:7, 13), (c) the "redemption" of Jesus' blood buying us back into God's favor (1 Peter 1:18-19), and (d) the "rejection" of Jesus as an example of how to handle mistreatment (1 Peter 2:20-24; 3:18; 4:1). Jesus. Jesus. Jesus. It was all about Jesus!

Peter pointed people to Jesus in the letter we call 2 Peter. He wrote this letter to warn his brethren about "false teachers" secretly and selfishly spreading "destructive heresies" about Jesus (2 Peter 2:1-3). To warn them, he used some form of the word *knowledge* sixteen times and coupled the word *Savior* with the words *Jesus Christ*. (That's more than anywhere else in the Bible.) And that's what was needed to combat the destructive opinions in circulation. They needed to know that Jesus Christ is our Savior. So Peter encouraged them to grow in their knowledge of our Lord (2 Peter 3:18). Again, he couldn't say enough about Jesus.

His nickname? Jesus gave him his nickname. In Aramaic, it's "Cephas," and in Greek, it's "Peter" (John 1:42). It means "rock," and I think it's safe to say that God had to do a lot of chiseling to make something out of that "rock." But all that hard work paid off, didn't it? Why do you think there was such a change in Peter's life? I have a theory. See what you think.

After he denied Jesus three times, a rooster crowed and, Luke tells us, "the Lord turned and looked at Peter" (Luke 22:61). The word translated *looked* carries the idea of Jesus staring at Peter. Can you imagine how difficult that was for Peter… how disappointing for Jesus? That's when Peter went out and wept like a baby (Luke 22:61-62). On the Sunday following, an angel announced the Lord's resurrection to a group of women and commissioned them to go "tell his disciples and Peter" (Matthew 28:1-7; Mark 16:7). *And Peter*?! Think of what those words must have meant to this man.

Here's something else: After Jesus met with two disciples walking toward the city of Emmaus, those same two disciples went to the apostles and said, "The Lord has risen indeed, and has appeared to Simon" (Luke 24:34). *Appeared to Simon*?! Wonder what that visit was about? Wonder what they talked about? Reckon it had something to do with shame, grace, forgiveness, and the real reason he was given his nickname? By the grace of God, he became what he was meant to be, "the Rock," a powerhouse for the Lord.

Rahab. Samson. Mary. Peter. These are just four of the many portraits we find on display inside God's "Showcase of Grace."

Oh, there are two more. Look carefully. There's a picture of…of you, or an empty frame where yours could be. See it? There's one of me too. That's true because we both need to echo those wonderful words of Paul:

> But by the grace of God I am what I am.
> 1 Corinthians 15:10

3

THE TASTE OF GRACE
Why Is Grace So Special?

Have you ever tasted that corky stuff between the meat of a pecan? It's nasty! Bitter. Ever bit into the wedge of a lemon? I dare you to try without making a funny face. It's sour. What comes to mind when you sink your front teeth into a popsicle right out of the freezer? "Agony! What was I thinking?!" It hurts. What happens when you take a big swallow of spoiled milk? Get out the paper towels. It's awful!

Now, compare all of that to a stack of buttermilk pancakes with hot maple syrup. Or a crisp piece of fried chicken with mashed potatoes and gravy. Or—if you're really country—a heapin' bowl of white beans and ham hock.

What do you think grace tastes like? I know that sounds like another off-the-wall question, but the Holy Spirit said,

> [A]s newborn babes, desire the pure milk of the word, that you may grow thereby, if indeed you

have *tasted* that the Lord is *gracious*.
> 1 Peter 2:2-3; emphasis mine

Our wonderful God is described in many ways. He's a "God of glory" (Acts 7:2), a "God of endurance and encouragement" (Romans 15:5), a "God of hope" (Romans 15:13), a "God of peace" (Romans 15:33), a "God of all comfort" (2 Corinthians 1:3), and a "God of love" (2 Corinthians 13:11). But my all-time favorite comes from the Holy Spirit-inspired words of Peter. God is "the God of all grace" (1 Peter 5:10). He's not the God of some grace. He's the God of "all grace."

God is the most gracious host we'll ever know, and the blessings that flow directly from his heart prove why grace is so special.

So let's pretend. Let's play like we've stepped inside a fancy restaurant that is owned by God. It's not a deli, where we can get a quick snack. It's not a little bistro with limited seating. It's not a buffet that allows us to pick what we want and eat all we can. This is one of those swanky places with napkins folded like tents and more silverware than we know what to do with. (I mean, who needs four forks?)

Gabriel, God's angelic messenger, is our table server. Pretty cool, huh!? He cordially offers us a menu. We don't get to select anything. He just shows it to us and explains how blessed we're about to be. We look over the menu. It's a fabulous multi-course meal. It has an incredible:

1. Appetizer — God's "Word of Life,"

2. Main Course — Jesus' "Abundant Life," and
3. Dessert — Hope's "Eternal Life"

Hungry? Let's dive in and see what God's grace tastes like.

THE APPETIZER

Most restaurants these days offer a selection of dishes that are served before the main course. Fried mozzarella. Stuffed mushrooms. Spinach and artichoke pastries. Chips and dip.

Along those lines, we might think of the Bible as the "appetizer" God has prepared for us before his main course. And, sure enough, this appetizer is the product of his grace.

> And now I commend you to God and to the *word of his grace*, which is able to build you up and to give you the inheritance among all those who are sanctified.
>
> Acts 20:32; emphasis mine

Did you see how the Bible is described? It's God's *word of grace*. The Bible is the miracle of all miracles. It's a book that came from the mind of God (1 Corinthians 2:10-13) with words that were breathed from the heart of God (2 Timothy 3:16). That's why it is called *the word of his grace* and *the gospel of the grace of God* (Acts 14:3; 20:24). It's here because of God's mercy, God's love, and God's kindness.

Can you think of life without it? It's "the word of life" that offers us an abundant life here and eternal life hereafter (Philippians 2:16). That's why we're thinking of it as a tasty appetizer. We must have it to enjoy the rest of God's banquet.

The Old Testament is part of this tasty appetizer in God's feast of faith. It gets us ready for the coming of our Savior (Luke 24:25, 44). For hundreds of years, God inspired men—prophets—to write about our Lord. Because of that, we can study Jesus' life, compare it to what the prophets predicted, and know beyond doubt that he really is our Savior (Acts 10:43).

The Old Testament also prepares us for the salvation our Savior offers (2 Timothy 3:16; 1 Peter 1:10-11). It alerts us to Jesus' coming and the importance of doing what he says (Deuteronomy 18:15, 18-19; Acts 3:22-23).

The New Testament is also a part of this tasty appetizer in God's feast of faith. It's that part of the Bible that introduces us to Jesus as the Savior God sent into the world (Matthew 1:18-25; cf. John 3:16-18; 1 John 4:14) and proves beyond measure that he's the Son of God we should believe in and obey (John 20:30-31; cf. Acts 10:38).

The New Testament also teaches us what to do to be saved and added to God's spiritual family (Romans 1:16). We start our path of becoming God's child by believing in Jesus (John 1:12). Then, we must repent and separate from the way we've been living (2 Corinthians 6:17-18) and be baptized into Jesus (Galatians 3:26-27).

So the Bible gets us ready for everything God has for us to enjoy in this world and beyond this world.

The Library of Congress has 838 miles of bookshelves. Yep. You read that right. 838 miles! It's the largest library in the world, boasting a collection of almost forty million books. 40,000,000! But all of those books combined can't equal the value of one Bible. Just one. Not one of those books can do what the Bible does for us.

- It's *the word of faith* that crafts our belief system (Romans 10:8).
- It's *the word of reconciliation* that secures our relationship with God (2 Corinthians 5:19),
- It's *the word of truth* that can be trusted at all times (2 Timothy 2:15).
- It's *the word of righteousness* that helps us be/do what's right (Hebrews 5:13-14).
- It's *the word of exhortation* that lifts us up when life knocks us down (Hebrews 13:22).

It's the book of all books, and it's here because our God is a God of grace.

THE MAIN COURSE

For the main course of a good meal, there's a "featured dish" and, then, "side items" to go with it. For example, we might have steak with a baked potato and green beans or asparagus. (Okay, that crazy-looking green stuff is a stretch.) For pork chops, we could enjoy a sweet potato, cinnamon apples, and a house salad. If we're having fish, it has to be hush puppies or fries (with catsup and hot sauce) and a generous helping of coleslaw (or, for the more sophisticated pallet, broccoli).

God's feast of faith is no different. Our gracious host has provided for us a great "featured dish" and some wonderful "side items" to go with it. Together, they make for what Jesus called an "abundant life" (John 10:10), or what Peter described as a life made possible by grace.

> Likewise, husbands, live with your wives in an understanding way, showing honor to the woman as the weaker vessel, since they are heirs with you of the *grace of life*.
>
> 1 Peter 3:7; emphasis mine

Jesus is the "featured dish" in God's feast of faith. He's from grace (Hebrews 2:9). He brought grace (John 1:17). He offers grace (Romans 3:24; 5:15). And, when he comes again, guess what he's bringing with him? Grace (1 Peter 1:13). There's never been anyone like him! That's why we are thinking of Jesus as the primary dish on the banquet table of God's blessings.

*Our Lord's **birth** was the special product of grace.* He wasn't here anytime until that was made known. Go back and slowly read through Luke 2. To begin, an angel announced Jesus' birth, calling him "Savior," "Christ," and "Lord" (vv. 9-14). Then, the Holy Spirit inspired an older gentleman named Simeon to see Jesus as the hope of our "salvation" (vv. 25-32). There was also a sweet, older prophetess named Anna, who recognized Jesus as the secret to our "redemption" (vv. 36-38). Angels of God. A Spirit-inspired man of God. A prophetess of God. And they all attested to the marvel of a little baby named Jesus. And, why was he born? To bring us grace!

> [He] *became flesh* and dwelt among us, and we have seen his glory, glory as of the only Son from the Father, *full of grace* and truth.
>
> John 1:14; emphasis mine

*Our Lord's **life** was the special product of grace.* Before he was born, he was "with God" (John 1:1-3; cf. Philippians 2:5-8). After he was born, he was "Immanuel," God with us (Matthew 1:23). He came to be the "light" that directs us to God (John 1:1-5) and the sacrificial "Lamb" that connects us back with God (John 1:29; cf. 1 Peter 1:18-19). Those who loved him called him: "Rabbi," "Messiah," "Christ," "the Son of God," and "the King of Israel" (John 1:35-49). He must have been an incredible person to be with.

- I'm amazed by the way *he harnessed his thoughts*. Jesus "knew no sin" (2 Corinthians 5:21). That means he never had bad feelings about anybody. He was lied to (e.g., John 4:17-18). He was lied about (e.g., Matthew 12:22-24). He was made out to be a liar (Luke 23:1-2; cf. Matthew 27:39-43). But he's the one that taught people to forgive and never carry a grudge (Mark 11:25-26). That's hard to fathom.

- I'm equally amazed by the way *he handled his temptations*. Jesus was tempted "in every respect…as we are, yet without sin" (Hebrews 4:15). That means he never caved to any of his appetites. Food? Jesus never struggled with an eating disorder (not wishing to disparage any of us who do). Drink? Jesus never stared down the cravings of one trying to live without alcohol (not wanting to judge any of us that might). Sex? Jesus' ministry was never tarnished by scandal or even the hint of impropriety (not meaning to be harsh toward any among us that have). In some way, to some degree, our Lord was tempted with all of that. But he lived without yielding to any of it as the "Holy and Righteous One" (Acts 3:14; cf. Mark 1:24). Isn't that something?!

- I'm also amazed by the way *he held his tongue*. When Jesus "was reviled, he did not revile in return" (1 Peter 2:22-23). That means he never said a bad word to those doing bad things to hurt him. He was called some of the worst things an orthodox Jew could imagine: e.g., a demon (John 7:20), a demon-possessed Samaritan (John 8:48), and even an insane demoniac to whom no one should pay attention (John 10:20). He was blasphemed, mocked, and reviled (Matthew 27:39-44). But others heard only words of kindness from him (e.g., Luke 23:34). Inspiring. Right?!

He never did anything wrong. *Nothing.* He never hosted a bad thought. He never did what he shouldn't have done. He never failed to do what he should have done. He lived every day

THE TASTE OF GRACE

just the way God wanted him to live. Why? Why did he leave everything in heaven to struggle on earth? Grace!

> [We] know the *grace* of our Lord Jesus Christ, that though he was rich, yet for your sake *he became poor*, so that you by his poverty might become rich.
> 2 Corinthians 8:9; emphasis mine

*Our Lord's **death** was also the special product of grace.* Crucifixion. Mutilation. Asphyxiation. Jesus' death was *despicable* and thought to be that of one "cursed" by God (Galatians 3:13; cf. Isaiah 53:3-4). Jesus' death was *shameful*, and for that reason, the Holy Spirit tells us he "endured the cross, despising the shame" (Hebrews 12:2). Jesus' death was *brutal*, a death of "hostility" and "bloodshed" (Hebrews 12:3-4). A scourging turned his back into confetti. Nails stapled his hands to a *stipes* (horizontal crossbeam) and his feet to a *patibulum* (vertical stake). He was left exposed to the elements, insects, and birds of prey. His heart was pierced with one barbed insult after another. We might also say that Jesus' death was *final*. He died. I know he was raised. But, still, he died. He breathed his final breath. His spirit was siphoned from his body. He journeyed to Hades, and his body was buried (Acts 2:31). Why? One word sums it all up. Grace!

> Jesus, [was] crowned with glory and honor because of the *suffering of death*, so that by the *grace* of God he might *taste death* for everyone.
> Hebrews 2:9; emphasis mine

With Jesus comes a variety of "side items" in God's feast of faith. Have you ever counted all the gifts that come from God? Unwrap them, and you'll have to agree with Joseph Oatman's nineteenth-century lyrics:

> Count your many blessings, name them one by one,
> And it will surprise you what the Lord hath done.

There is: (a) the "gift of the Holy Spirit" (Acts 5:32), (b) the "gift of righteousness" (Romans 5:17), and (c) the "gift of eternal life" (Romans 6:23; Ephesians 2:8). "Every good gift and every perfect gift is from above, coming down from the Father of lights" (James 1:17), and several of them are mentioned right alongside grace. That's why we like to think of them as the "side items" we enjoy with God's banquet of blessings.

First, with Jesus, there is the "side item," or blessing, of forgiveness. To me, it's the greatest gift God has ever given. Think about it. The Bible was written to tell us about forgiveness (1 Corinthians 15:1-2). Jesus was sent to offer us forgiveness (1 John 4:9-10). The Holy Spirit is given to us when we receive forgiveness (Acts 2:38). We're right with God because we have forgiveness (Romans 6:18). And, eternal life will be ours if we're among the forgiven, the justified [just-if-I'd never sinned] (Titus 3:7). Forgiveness allows us back into God's heart, but that is only because of something that came from God's heart. Grace!

> Blessed be the God and Father of our Lord Jesus Christ, who has blessed us in Christ with every spiritual blessing in the heavenly places...In him

> we have redemption through his blood, the *forgiveness* of our trespasses, *according to the riches of his grace.*
>
> Ephesians 1:3, 7; emphasis mine

Second, with Jesus, there is the "side item," or blessing, of **prayer**. Prayer can make a huge difference in the way we live. It helps us: (a) live without worry (Philippians 4:6-7), (b) be more thoughtful (Colossians 4:2), (c) love those that hurt us (Matthew 5:44), (d) be a better citizen (1 Timothy 2:1-2), (e) deepen our trust in God (James 5:13), and (f) strengthen the bond we share with each other (James 5:16). It "has great power as it is working" (James 5:16). Why?

- With prayer, we get God's *attention* (1 Peter 3:12).
- With prayer, we have Jesus' *mediation* (Hebrews 7:25; 9:24; cf. 1 Timothy 2:1-5).
- With prayer, we are blessed with the Holy Spirit's *intercession* (Romans 8:26-27).
- And with prayer, the Godhead responds to our requests by doing what is best, something we might call providential *intervention* (Matthew 7:7-11).

Prayer is personal. It can change us. Prayer is powerful. It can change our circumstances. And, guess what makes prayer such a blessing. How'd you guess? Grace!

> Let us then with confidence *draw near* to the throne

of *grace*, that we may receive mercy and find *grace* to help in time of need.

Hebrews 4:16; emphasis mine

*Third, with Jesus, there is the "side item," or blessing, of **peace**.* Edward Henry Bickersteth Jr., a bishop in the Church of England, penned these lyrics more than one hundred years ago:

Peace, perfect peace, in this dark world of sin?
The blood of Jesus whispers peace within.

They still resonate and remind us of how blessed we are to be forgiven and live in perfect harmony with God (1 John 1:7-10). Forgiven of all our "yesterdays." Forgiven today. Forever forgiven as long as we continue to walk with God. How's that for "peace"?! And grace is what makes that possible.

[S]ince we have been justified by faith, we have *peace with God* through our Lord Jesus Christ. Through him we have also obtained access by faith into this *grace in which we stand*, and we rejoice in hope of the glory of God.

Romans 5:1-2; emphasis mine

THE DESSERT

"Can I interest you in dessert?" How many times have we heard that question? It comes at the end of the main course. We're offered the good stuff that tops off the glorious meal we've already enjoyed. A lot of times, the restaurant has a special dessert that only it is known for. And we're encouraged to think about that dessert before or during our meal. There are usually pictures of some scrumptious dish and a description that drips with calories. (I mean, I can gain three pounds just reading about it.) Of course, our table server constantly reminds us to save room for it.

God's banquet of blessings has a special dessert as well.

Hope of eternal life is the *dessert* that comes with God's feast of faith. Two glorious thoughts are combined in scripture to help us see what hope means:

- First, biblical hope is the desire or *anticipation* of something. Solomon put it this way: "Hope deferred makes the heart sick, but a desire fulfilled is a tree of life (Proverbs 13:12). Did you see how he used "hope" and "desire" as synonyms? Isn't that neat?

- Second, biblical hope is the *anticipation* of something. Solomon also wrote, "The hope of the righteous brings joy, but the expectation of the wicked will perish" (Proverbs 10:28; cf. 11:7). This time, he used "hope" and "expectation" interchangeably.

So, hope is wanting something and expecting to receive that something. When Paul wrote about the "hope of eternal life, which God, who never lies, promised before the ages began" (Titus 1:2), he was writing about something we want and something we can expect as Christians. We want to and we expect to live with God eternally at the end of our life's main course. And, why will that be possible? Grace!

> Now may our Lord Jesus Christ himself, and God our Father, who loved us and gave us eternal comfort and good *hope* through *grace*, comfort your hearts and establish them.
> 2 Thessalonians 2:16-17; emphasis mine

Hope of eternal life is also the *specialty dessert* that comes with God's feast of faith. It's something only God can offer up. And, folks, according to Revelation 21, it's the good stuff!

- Think about the *location* of heaven. We'll get to be with God, and God has promised to be with us (vv. 1-3).

- Think about the *attention* of heaven. We'll know the care of God…no more tears, death, sorrow, crying, or pain (vv. 4-6).

- Think about the *population* of heaven. We'll be surrounded by winners, those who fought and overcame for God (vv. 7-8).

- Think about the *fascination* of heaven. We'll be in the home that belongs to God, with all of its regal glory and splendor (vv. 9-27).

- Think about the *duration* of heaven (even though it is not specifically mentioned in Revelation 21). It is, after all, "eternal life" (Matthew 25:46)!

As Christians, we not only want to go there, we expect to go there. That's what it means to hope for eternal life. And that assurance is ours; that's right, it's ours because of God's grace!

> [B]eing justified by his *grace* we…[are] heirs according to the *hope of eternal life*.
> Titus 3:7; emphasis mine

Maybe you've seen the signs. They're designed to keep some people away.

"NO SHOES. NO SHIRT. NO SERVICE."

You'll never see anything like that when it comes to God's feast of faith.

His "appetizer," the word he has given to prepare us for our Savior, is a word for all of us (Mark 16:15; Romans 1:16-17).

His "main course," the Savior he has sent to repair us and grant us a life that is a life indeed, is a Savior he sent for all of us (Titus 2:11; Hebrews 2:9).

His "dessert," the salvation he has offered us, is a salvation he's provided for all of us (1 Timothy 4:10; Hebrews 5:9).

"No shoes. No shirt. No service." No. The sign outside God's banquet of blessings is far more *gracious*. It goes something like this:

> The Spirit and the Bride say, "Come." And let the one who hears say, "Come." And let the one who is thirsty come; let the one who desires take the water of life without price.
>
> Revelation 22:17

When someone asks, "What does that taste like?", one of two answers is generally given. There's the *classic*: "It tastes like chicken." Then, there's the *colossal*: "It taste like nothing you've ever put in your mouth." Grace is like the latter. It's an exquisite delicacy for which there is no comparison. It fills us up and satisfies in ways we can't even express. At the same time, it leaves us wanting more. We can't ever get enough, hear enough, or praise God enough for it. It's that special. The psalmist has said it best:

> Because your steadfast love [i.e., grace] is better than life, my lips will praise you. So I will bless you as long as I live; in your name I will lift up my hands. My soul will be satisfied as with fat and rich food, and my mouth will praise you with joyful lips...
>
> Psalm 63:3-5

4

THE DISGRACE OF GRACE
Will Grace Overlook My Behavior?

I'm going to go out on a limb and say there are two things neither one of us like.

First of all, I hate it when someone *takes me for granted*. They treat me like I'm nothing more than a light switch. You know, like I'm someone that's always going to be there. Someone that's always going to work when they need me to. Someone to whom they have to give very little thought. They never give me a word of encouragement, no matter how encouraging I try to be. *Thank you* isn't in their vocabulary. *How are you feeling?* is a question they don't know how to ask. They look over me, work around me, and treat me as if I don't even exist. Know the feeling?

I also hate it when someone *takes advantage of me*. They treat me like I'm a pawn on the checkerboard of their own wishes. What they want, I'm supposed to want. Their thoughts are supposed to be my thoughts. They even dare to think for me:

"He won't mind." How do they know?! "I know him," they say. "It'll be all right." Wrong! They make me want to stand up and scream, "Wait a minute! My universe doesn't revolve around you!" Can you relate?

I don't think I'm selfish...but I'm not a shellfish either! I have feelings. And I want them to be respected. Hey, I want to be respected. Don't you? God does. And that brings us to the last chapter of our study.

God has feelings too. Remember? That's what grace is all about: his mercy, his love, and his kindness. And, this is something we don't always think about. God wants his feelings to be respected. Jesus said, "Not everyone who says to me, 'Lord, Lord,' will enter the kingdom of heaven, but the one who does the will of my Father who is in heaven" (Matthew 7:21).

But some of us *take God's feelings for granted*. And others of us *take advantage of God's feelings*. We disgrace his grace by living as if there are:

1. No Rules...keeping us from doing what we want to do, or

2. Nothing But Rules...keeping us from doing what we could do.

For our last chapter together, let's think about the possibility of our abusing God's grace with these two extremes.

Got your scuba gear on? Tanks full? We may be diving a little deeper than we have in some of our previous studies, but trust me, the treasure we'll find is worth the effort.

NO RULES

Archimedes was a third-century mathematician, physicist, engineer, and astronomer. He's credited for inventing the catapult, the compound pulley, and some of the original contributions to geometry. It's said that he anticipated the infinitesimals of calculus before Isaac Newton and Gottfried Leibniz discovered the discipline fourteen hundred years later. Archimedes is the one that is supposed to have said, "Give me a place to stand, and I will move the world."

I've heard it said that we'll either *move the world* or we'll be *moved by the world*. We'll either have a positive impact on others, or others will have a negative impact on us. It's clear which of the two God wants. He has said, "Do not be conformed to this world" (Romans 12:2). He's given us a warning: "Do you not know that friendship with the world is enmity with God?" (James 4:4). And, we've been told emphatically, "Do not love the world or the things in the world. If anyone loves the world, the love of the Father is not in him" (1 John 2:15).

I fear that it's easier for some of us to be influenced than it is for us to have an influence. We'd rather blend than contend with our culture. We don't have the heart to be different and stand apart. The results are telling:

- We used to dress like "ole Mother Hubbard," but today, we dress like her cupboard, *bare*.
- We act like adultery is the *adult* thing to do.
- We live as if the *Im* of *Immorality* stands for the morality *I'm* going to choose.

- We have to confess that stress has made a mess of us because we address life without God.
- We're in the world, and unfortunately, too much of the world is in us.

Still, we want a relationship with God. So we try to make it okay for us to disobey. We think, "It's all right for me to do whatever I want to do…God will have feelings for me anyway." We take his feelings for granted and disgrace his grace.

It might be good for us to revisit the questions Paul asked in Romans 6. There are four of them, and they are presented as couplets of thought (Romans 6:1, 15).

> What shall we say then? Are we to continue in sin that grace may abound?

> What then? Are we to sin because we are not under law but under grace?

Look at the *pronoun* Paul used in these questions. He brought himself into the discussion. "Are *we* to continue in sin? Are *we* to sin?" A study of grace would be incomplete if we failed to see the change it brought to the life of Paul. He's the one that said, "[F]ormerly I was a blasphemer, persecutor, and insolent opponent. But I received mercy…and the grace of our Lord overflowed for me" (1 Timothy 1:13-14).

Before Paul became a Christian, he was: (a) a *blasphemer* who said hateful things about Jesus and tried to get others to talk that way (Acts 26:9-11); (b) a *persecutor* who threatened and murdered those who followed Jesus (Acts 9:1); and (c) an *insolent opponent* who violently tried to destroy the church of Jesus (Acts 9:21; Galatians 1:12-14).

Could Paul keep on saying ugly things after he became a Christian? Could he continue to destroy lives? Could he maintain his efforts to exterminate the church? Could he continue to live as if there were no rules keeping him from doing what he had been doing or what he wanted to do? That's the gist of what he was asking.

Look at the *unsound* concept Paul referenced in these questions. The verbs he used paint an interesting word picture: "Are we to *continue in sin* (literally, "stay on sin") that grace may abound?...*Are* we to *sin* (literally, "Are we to keep on sinning?")?" They suggest the idea of someone continuing to walk down a path of sin and continuing to sin so that God can be who God is...i.e., merciful, loving, and kind.

That whole notion smacks in the face of what God says in the rest of Romans 6 about: (a) *repentance* being the death of the person I used to be (vv. 1-2) and (b) *baptism* being the line between the dead-and-buried person I used to be and the changed person I am to be (vv. 3-4), as well as (c) *the new life* I should be trying to live (vv. 5-6).

There's just no way we can keep on doing what we wish, as if there were no rules to restrict our behavior. We died to our past, and we're not to be "instruments of unrighteousness" anymore. We are to be "instruments of righteousness" for God (v. 13). That's why we're told to live apart from our past. "*[P]ut off*, concerning your former conduct, the *old man*…and be *renewed* in the spirit of your mind…*put on the new man*" (Ephesians 4:20-24; emphasis mine).

Look at the *profound* answer Paul gave to these questions. Can we keep on doing what we've been doing because God is gracious? Can we keep on sinning? The answer to both questions is the same. And it couldn't be more emphatic: "By no means" (vv. 2, 15). Other translations are just as forceful: "God forbid" (KJV and ASV), "Certainly not" (NKJV), "May it never be" (NASV), and "Absolutely not" (HCSB). Get the picture? We don't have the right to take God's feelings for granted and live like the world. God has feelings too, and they are to be deeply respected. We should never disgrace his grace by living like there are no rules to keep us from doing what we want to do.

Well, we've been swimming pretty deep. Want to come up for air? Okay. Let's take a breather…but hold on to that rich nugget we just found: "We cannot be who we want to be just because God is who God is, gracious."

NOTHING BUT RULES

All right. Break time is over. Let's dive back in. Get ready. This time we're going to go down even deeper. But, again, I believe, the wealth we'll come up with will be worth the struggle. So, here we go.

When I was a boy, there was a huge drainage ditch behind our house. A pipe ran from one side of the ditch to the other. It was probably ten inches in diameter, forty feet long, and a good eight feet off the ground. Guess what that pipe looked like to an eight-year-old? A dare! A double-dog dare.

It taunted me when I came to the edge of the ditch. It haunted me when I walked away. Should I? Could I? What would happen if I tried to walk across that pipe from one side to the other? When I finally got the nerve to try…well, let's just say it wasn't all that pretty. But, you know what? After a while, I could not only walk across the pipe, I could run across it without even looking. Want to know the secret? "Courage," you say. No. "Confidence." Nope. The secret was: balance.

Ever had one of your car tires get out of balance? It makes for a rough ride. Have you ever put your forehead on the handle of a baseball bat, run in circles around the bat, and then tried to walk away in a straight line? It's crazy. You can't. No balance!! What happens when you stand on the edge of a cliff and look over? If you're like me, you don't want to lean too far or look too long. You'll feel like you're about to fall. The height distorts your perception and takes away your sense of balance.

Christianity—true Christianity—is a religion of balance.

- Our God is a "caring Father" and a "consuming fire" (Hebrews 12:9-11, 29; cf. 10:26-29).
- Our Savior is a "Lion" and a "Lamb" (Revelation 5:5-12).
- Our Guide, the Holy Spirit, "dwells in" us, and he expects us to "dwell in" him, in his teachings (Romans 8:8-9).
- Our Bibles are full of "milk" and "meat," "precepts" and "promises" (Hebrews 5:12-14; 2 Corinthians

6:16-7:1).

- Our Lord's church is a "family" of brethren, but it's also an "army" of soldiers (Philippians 1:25; cf. Philemon 1-2, 7).
- Our Christian walk is one supported by Bible-based "convictions" that are seasoned with "compassion" (1 Corinthians 16:13-14).

Sadly, we're a "people of the pendulum." We get imbalanced. We swing from one extreme to another and we are even that with grace. Some of us take God's feelings for granted and think we can do whatever we want because of his grace. Then, there are those of us who are guilty of the opposite extreme. We take advantage of God's feelings and treat him like he is here for us. We try to think for him and speak for him. Don't deny it. We do. We twist his word into saying what we want it to say to support our man-made piety. We turn our traditions into his truth to determine what is right, and then we think we are right by doing all that we say is right and doing it all in the right way. I know. It's hard to believe that there are people who think that way, but believe me, there are. To them, Christianity is all about "the rules." (And it's usually the ones they deem more important than others…or the ones they make up).

They'd be the first to tell you it's impossible to earn your salvation, but at the same time, they're living like they have to… and they expect everyone else to as well. "Do what is right, do it in the right way, and that's the way to be right with God," is their idea. Their relationship with God hinges more on *what they are doing* for God than on *what God has done or is doing* for them through Jesus. This mindset makes us legalists who disgrace the grace of God.

If you've struggled with that like I have, you need to consider what Paul had to say in the book of Galatians. At one time, Paul thought like that, but after he became a Christian, he wanted nothing to do with that mindset. Listen to him:

> I do not *nullify the grace* of God, for if righteousness were through the *law* [more literally, "through law," a legalistic system of "dos" and "don'ts"], then Christ died for no purpose.
> Galatians 2:21; emphasis mine

> You are severed from Christ, you who would be justified by the *law* [literally, again, "by law," a legalistic system of "dos" and "don'ts"]; you have *fallen away from grace*.
> Galatians 5:4; emphasis mine

According to Paul, heartless rule-keeping will *nullify* the grace of God. The word he used for *nullify* could also be translated as *displace* or *reject*. If we think we can be right with God by rule-keeping, we reject his grace. It's like we're thinking we don't need his grace. We don't need God…God needs us. *Really*?! Trying to be right with God based on our own merit isn't right. In fact, it's not even possible.

The Old Testament was a rule-keeping system of law. "Thou shalt…do this." "Thou shalt not…don't do that." As a result, it demanded perfect obedience: "For all who rely on works of the law are under a curse; for it is written, 'Cursed be everyone who does not abide by all things written in the Book of the Law, and do them'" (Galatians 3:10).

Prior to his conversion, that's how Paul tried to live. He thought he was right with God because of everything he was doing and the way he was doing everything. He said, "[I was] of the tribe of Benjamin, a Hebrew of Hebrews; as to the law, a Pharisee; as to zeal, a persecutor of the church; as to righteousness under the law, blameless" (Philippians 3:5-6).

Paul was proud of himself and his religious heritage. He was: (a) *of the tribe of Benjamin*, the elite of Israel; (b) *a Hebrew of Hebrews* that could trace his lineage back to Abraham through Jacob instead of Esau; (c) *a Pharisee and blameless* when it came to the law, which means he was a strict, arrogant, "nitpickin'" legalist (Acts 26:5); and (d) *a persecutor of the church* as a result. He had the "righteousness" of a law system and thought he was "right" with God (Act 23:1). Was he? Remember what Jesus asked him on the road to Damascus: "Why are you persecuting me?" (Acts 9:4). With all that rule-keeping, he thought he was right, but he couldn't have been more wrong.

According to Paul, heartless rule-keeping will *vilify* the character of God. If we can be right with God based on our own merit, "then Christ died for no purpose." The word translated *no purpose* is rendered "without a cause" elsewhere (John 15:25). Wow. Think about that. If we can please God by our own rule-keeping, there was "no cause" for Jesus to go through all the trauma of Calvary.

Why did God send Jesus in the first place? He "loved us and sent his Son to be the propitiation for our sins" (1 John 4:9-10). Break that passage down. (a) God loved us. (b) God sent his Son for us. (c) God loved us and sent his Son for us so that he could be pleased with us again. That's the meaning of *propitiation*. But if we can keep the right amount of rules in the right way and please God on our own, none of that had to happen.

That means God didn't have to send Jesus and make him go through the awful hostility of Golgotha. But he did. That turns God's gift of compassion into a gesture of cruelty. If we can be right with God on our own, Jesus was *double-crossed* by God when he was sent to *the cross*. He was betrayed by a God who sent him to do something he didn't have to do. That makes God *mean* rather than *merciful* and *vicious* instead of *gracious*.

According to Paul, heartless rule-keeping, will, once again, *crucify* the Son of God. Too many of us are like those in Galatia. We try to be justified by a rule-keeping system more than a system of faith that motivates us to obey God out of love. "[W]e know that a person is not justified by works of the law but through faith in Jesus Christ" (Galatians 2:16; cf. 3:11). We know that, but we try to be justified by our rule-keeping anyway. We know that obedience is the product of love (1 John 5:3; cf. John 14:15), but we turn it into doing what we've been told to do simply because it's what we've been told to do.

You know what this kind of thinking does to us? Look at Paul's words again: "You are severed from Christ, you who would be justified by the law [literally, "by law," a legalistic system of "dos" and "don'ts"]; you have fallen away from grace"

(Galatians 5:4). Three things happen: (a) We are not where we used to be because we've been *severed*. (b) We are not with Jesus anymore because we've been severed from (literally, "away from") *Christ*. (c) And we have *fallen from* (more literally, "out of") *grace*. Yes, we can fall from grace. We can fall away from the benefits we once enjoyed, the blessings that came to us from God's mercy, love, and kindness. And that's what happens when we try to justify ourselves by some kind of heartless, rule-keeping system of "do" this and "don't do" that.

You know what this kind of thinking does to Jesus? When we fall away, we find ourselves "crucifying once again the Son of God…and holding him up to contempt" (Hebrews 6:4-6). We slap him in the face. We spit on his person. We pull the beard from his cheeks. We nail his hands and feet to the cross. We hurl insults of bitterness and blasphemy. How? Why? We do so by falling away, and we fall away when we treat him like we don't need him. After all, we're doing what's right…in the right way…and that's why we're right. Horrible, isn't it?!

Okay, let's surface. Now, we have another priceless nugget to cherish: "We cannot heartlessly comply to a set of rules—do this/don't do that—and think we're right on our own merit. We need God. We need his grace! We need everything his grace is and everything his grace makes possible."

Over the door of my study, I've placed a sign. The paint color of the room may change. The furniture may be updated on occasion. Bookshelves and books may be added. But that sign is always there. I think you'd like it. It's on the inside, so you'll have to come in and visit if you want to see it. It melts my heart every time I read it, think on it, or pray about it.

In His grasp. By His grace. For His glory.

Can you think of anything more comforting than our being in the hands of a caring Father? Can you wrap your mind around anything more captivating than the gracious heart of God Almighty? Is there any thought more inspiring than the possibility of our being able to bring him glory?

Our wants should be what God wants. What God wants should be what we want…because we believe in him and love him. Why would we ever want to take God's feelings for granted—thinking it's all right to do what we wish? Why would we ever want to take advantage of God's feelings—thinking we're all right simply because we're doing everything the right way?

If we really believe in the God of the Bible, if we really love him with all of our hearts, all of our souls, and all of our minds (Matthew 22:37), why would we ever dream of pursuing any extreme that would "Disgrace his Grace"?!

Thank you for sharing some of your study time. I hope you've found our thoughts to be helpful. I pray that they have encouraged you to think a little more about someone who thinks of you all the time: our *gracious* heavenly Father. So, until we're blessed to study together again, here's my prayer for us:

> Let the favor [i.e., the grace] of the Lord our God be upon us, and establish the work of our hands.
> Psalm 90:17

ACKNOWLEDGMENTS

Gratitude is a debt we owe the kindness of others. As we come to the close of another wonderful study, I feel indebted to so many.

Let me begin with words of praise for Michael Whitworth, owner and president of Start2Finish. Years separate our dates of birth but our hearts seem to beat as one. Michael, once again, thank you for your encouragement, your commitment to excellence, your sterling counsel and, even more, your friendship. You keep my thoughts young. You constantly inspire me to grow. You motivate me to dream. I love you with the heart of Jesus.

Brandon Jackson and Brandon Edwards of Hidden Bridge Media—along with the tireless craftsmanship of William Bush—have, once again, crafted twelve beautiful videos to accompany this book and its twelve-lesson Study Guide companion. Fellows, you've heard me say it many times, but I can't say it enough. Thank you for being who you are: creative, professional, perfectionists…beloved brothers in the Lord. We've worked together on several projects, and you never fail to amaze me. You have been blessed but, to me, you're a blessing.

I wish to thank Katie Gilchrist for serving as my editor. You can't read her last name without seeing the word "Christ," and I really appreciate the unique way she blends her editing skills with her love for Christ. Katie, thank you for placing each word, phrase, and sentence of this study under the magnifying glass of your loving attention. You're special.

On that same note, I'd like to take pause and thank one of those quiet, behind-the-scenes servants of Jesus. Sheri Glazier has the ominous responsibility of giving my words one last look before they make their way to the printer. Sheri, thank you for the incredible care you give to the smallest detail. Your special vision contributes so much to our mission: "Expose the heart of God to the world."

ABOUT THE AUTHOR

Dan Winkler has shared the story of Jesus on university campuses, in churches, convention centers, and living rooms across the U.S. His uncanny ability to unravel a biblical text and invite its meaning into our world makes him a terrific Bible study partner. You will find Dan's sensitive spirit and gentle wit to be a refreshing contribution to your pursuit of God. Dan teaches New Testament studies at Freed-Hardeman University in Henderson, Tennessee. He has preached the unsearchable riches of Christ since 1969. He and his wife, Diane, have been blessed with three sons and seven grandchildren.